Army Officer Interview Questions

www.How2Become.com

As part of this product you have also received FREE access to online tests that will help you to pass the Army Assessments:

To gain access, simply go to:

www.MyPsychometricTests.co.uk

Get more products for passing any test at:

www.How2Become.com

Orders: Please contact How2Become Ltd, Suite 14, 50 Churchill Square Business Centre, Kings Hill, Kent ME19 4YU.

You can order through Amazon.co.uk under ISBN: **9781909229655**, via the website www.How2Become.com or through Gardners.com.

ISBN: **9781909229655**

First published in 2014 by How2Become Ltd.

Updated in 2018.

Copyright © 2018 How2Become.

Typeset by Katie Noakes for How2Become Ltd.

Disclaimer

Every effort has been made to ensure that the information contained within this guide is accurate at the time of publication. How2Become Ltd is not responsible for anyone failing any part of any selection process as a result of the information contained within this guide. How2Become Ltd and their authors cannot accept any responsibility for any errors or omissions within this guide, however caused. No responsibility for loss or damage occasioned by any person acting, or refraining from action, as a result of the material in this publication can be accepted by How2Become Ltd.

The information within this guide does not represent the views of any third party service or organisation.

CONTENTS

INTRODUCTION

Welcome to your new guide – *How to Pass the Army Officer Interview*. This guide has been designed to help you prepare for the Army Officer interviews, including the Army Officer Selection Board. The guide contains lots of sample interview questions, answers and preparation advice that is suitable for both the Careers Advisor interview and also both sets of AOSB (Briefing and Main Board).

The author of this guide, Richard McMunn, has over twenty years combined experience in the Armed Forces and the Emergency Services. He has vast experience and knowledge in the area of Armed Forces recruitment and you will find his guidance both inspiring and highly informative. During his successful career in the Fire Service, Richard sat on many interview panels assessing candidates seeking to join the Service. He has also been extremely successful at passing job interviews and assessments himself, with a success rate of over 90%. Follow his advice and preparation techniques carefully and you too can achieve the same level of success in your career.

Whilst the selection process for joining the Army as an Officer is highly competitive, there are a number of things you can do to improve your chances of success, and they are all contained within this guide.

The guide itself has been split up into useful sections to make it easier for you to prepare for each stage. Read each section carefully and take notes as you progress. Don't ever give up on your dream; if you really want to join the Army as an Officer, then you can do it. The way to approach an application for a job in the Armed Forces is to embark on a programme of 'in-depth' preparation, and this guide will show you exactly how to do just that.

If you need any further help with the aptitude tests, planning exercises, getting fit or AOSB advice, then we offer a wide range of products to assist you. These are all available through our online shop www.how2become. com or online via Amazon.co.uk.

Once again thank you for your custom, and we wish you every success in your ambition of joining the Army.

Work hard, stay focused, and secure your dream career!

Best wishes,

The how2become team

CHAPTER 1
THE ARMY OFFICER INTERVIEW

During the selection process you will be required to sit interviews at both the Armed Forces Careers Office (AFCO) and during your attendance at the AOSB Briefing and Main Board.

Whilst the questions and tips contained within this section of the guide concentrate primarily on the AFCO interview, they are also great preparation for the AOSB, too. The initial interview, which is held at your local Armed Forces Careers Office, will be undertaken by a member of the Army recruitment team. The purpose of this interview is to 'filter' out those people who have the potential to join the Army as an Officer.

The duration of the initial AFCO interview will very much depend on your responses to the questions. However, you can expect the interview to last for approximately 30 minutes. The questions that you will be assessed against during the initial interview will normally be taken from the following areas:

- The reasons why you want to join the Army and why you have chosen this service over the Royal Navy or the Royal Air Force.

- Why you want to become an Officer and what skills, qualities and experiences you have that would help you to become either a competent Officer.

- What choice of career you are most interested in, the reason for choosing that career, and the skills you have to match the role.

- What information you already have about the Army, its history, its lifestyle and training.

- Information relating to your hobbies and interests including sporting/ team activities.

- Any personal responsibilities that you currently have at home, in your education or at work.

- Questions based around your ability to work as part of a team, leadership potential, confidence, resilience, planning, organising, communication skills, how you learn new skills or information and personal development.

- Information about your family and your partner and what they think about you joining.

- Information based around your initial application.

- Your experience of work and education.

- Your emotional stability and your maturity.

- Your drive and determination to succeed.

- Having a positive reaction to a disciplined environment and towards people in positions of authority.

Before we move on to a number of sample interview questions and tips for answering them, we want to explain a little bit about interview technique and how to come across in a positive manner during the interview.

As you can imagine, there will always be good applicants, and there will always be poor applicants.

Let us explain the difference between a good applicant and a poor one.

A GOOD APPLICANT

A good applicant is someone who has taken the time to prepare. They have researched both the organisation they are applying to join, and also the role that they are being interviewed for. They may not know every detail about the organisation and the role but it will be clear that they have made an effort to find out important facts and information. They will be well presented at the interview and they will be confident, but not over confident. As soon as they walk into the interview room they will be polite and courteous and they will sit down in the interview chair only when invited to do so. Throughout the interview they will sit upright in the chair and communicate in a positive manner. If they do not know the answer to a question they will say so and they won't try and waffle. At the end of the interview they will ask positive questions about the job or the organisation before shaking hands and leaving.

A POOR APPLICANT

A poor applicant could be any combination of the following. They will be late for the interview or even forget to turn up at all. They will have made little effort to dress smart and they will have carried out little or no preparation. When asked questions about the job or the organisation they will have little or no knowledge. Throughout the interview they will appear to be unenthusiastic about the whole process and will look as if they want the interview to be over as soon as possible. Whilst sat in the interview chair they will slouch and fidget. At the end of the interview they will try to ask clever questions that are intended to impress the panel.

INTERVIEW TECHNIQUE

How you present yourself during the interview is important. Whilst assessing candidates for interviews, we will not only assess their responses to the interview questions, but we will also pay attention to the way they present themselves. A candidate could give excellent responses to the interview questions, but if they present themselves in a negative manner, this can lose them marks.

In the build-up to your initial AFCO interview practise a few 'mock' interviews. Look to improve your interview technique as well as working on your responses to the interview questions.

Let's now take a look at some of the important areas you will be assessed against during the Army Officer interview.

- **Teamwork** – This could include examples of being a part of sports teams, group organisations and work. Ideally, competency examples should be within the last year.

- **Resilience** – You will be required to describe your physical fitness preparations. You need to demonstrate an understanding of the challenges of serving in the Army and how you have managed pressure in the past.

- **Problem Solving** – This should be a fairly recent example of when you have had to solve a problem and provide details of how you resolved the issue and what the outcome was. Examples could be from any activity you are involved in, including work.

- **Planning and Organising** – A recent event or activity that you have organised or planned. This is something that is fundamental to the role of Army Officer.

- **Learning and Developing** – You should have a good understanding of the Army and the job you want to do whilst serving, including the terms and conditions of service, training, roles, and why you are attracted to the Army in general and to your particular chosen job/career path. You could also be asked about how you enjoy learning things and what you have done recently to develop or improve yourself.

- **Discipline** – Looking at your interaction with people in authority and how you react to rules. What responsibilities do you currently have?

- **Communication Skills** – These will be assessed throughout the interview.

If I were preparing for the Army Officer interview right now I would take each of the above assessable areas individually, and prepare a detailed response setting out the extent to which I meet its requirements. Your response to each question that relates to the above competency areas must be 'specific' in nature. This means that you must provide an example in which you have already demonstrated the skills required for that area. Do not fall into the trap of providing a 'generic' response that details what you 'would do' if the situation arose.

Try to structure your responses in a logical and concise manner. The way to achieve this is to use the 'STAR' method of interview question response construction:

- ## SITUATION

Start off your response to the interview question by explaining what the 'situation' was and who was involved.

- ## TASK

Once you have detailed the situation, explain what the 'task' was, or what needed to be done.

- ## ACTION

Now explain what 'action' you took, and what action others took. Also explain why you took this particular course of action.

• RESULT

Explain what the outcome was following your actions and those of others. Try to demonstrate in your response that the outcome was positive as a result of the action you took.

Finally, explain to the panel what you would do differently if the same situation were to arise again. It is good to be reflective at the end of your responses. This demonstrates a level of maturity and it will also show the panel that you are willing to learn from every experience.

During the next section of the guide, we have specifically provided sample questions and answers that cover the above competency areas. The chapters thereafter will cover the more generic questions, and questions aimed at candidates preparing for the AOSB.

TEAM WORKING

It is very important that you are capable of working as part of a team when you join the Army. I will now provide you with a few relevant sample questions that I would encourage you to prepare for.

Sample Question

Tell me about a time when you have contributed to the effective working of a team.

How to structure your response:

• What was the size and purpose of the team?

• Who else was in the team?

• What was YOUR role in the team? (Explain your exact role.)

• What did you personally do to help make the team effective?

• What was the result?

STRONG RESPONSE

To make your response strong you need to provide specific details of where you have worked with others effectively, and more importantly where YOU have contributed to the team. Try to think of an example where there was a problem within a team and where you volunteered to make the team work more efficiently. It is better to say that you identified there was problem within the team rather than that you were asked to do something by your manager or supervisor. Make your response concise and logical.

WEAK RESPONSE

Those candidates who fail to provide a specific example will provide weak answers. Do not fall into the trap of saying 'what you would do' if this type of situation arose.

Sample Response

"I like to keep fit and healthy and as part of this aim I play football for a local Sunday team. We had worked very hard to get to the cup final and we were faced with playing a very good opposition team who had recently won the league title. The team consisted of eleven players who regularly spend time together during training sessions and at social events. After only ten minutes of play, one of our players was sent off and we conceded a penalty as a result. Being one goal down and 80 minutes left to play we were faced with a mountain to climb. However, we all remembered our training and worked very hard in order to prevent any more goals being scored. Due to playing with ten players, I had to switch positions and play as a defender, something that I am not used to. Apart from being a defender I felt my role was to encourage the other players to keep going and to not give up until the final whistle had sounded. All the other players supported each other tremendously and the support of the crowd really pushed us on. The team worked brilliantly to hold off any further opposing goals and after 60 minutes we managed to get an equaliser. The game went to penalties in the end and we managed to win the cup. I believe I am an excellent team player and can always be relied upon to work as an effective team member at all times. I understand that being an

effective team member is very important if the Army is to continually perform to a very high standard. However, above all of this, effective teamwork is essential in order to maintain the high safety standards that are set."

Sample Question

Do you have any experience of working as a team member?

The ability to work effectively in a team is an extremely important aspect of the role of Army personnel. Not only will you be spending a great deal of time together at work, you will also depend on your colleagues during highly dangerous and stressful incidents. Therefore, it is important that you can demonstrate you have the ability to work as an effective team member. Although as an Officer you will be required to lead your team, being able to also work as an effective team member is crucial.

When responding to this type of question, try to think of occasions when you have been part of a team and achieved a common goal.

Maybe you are already involved in team sports playing hockey, rugby or football? You may also find that you have experience of working as a team member through work. If you have no or very little experience of working as a team member then try to get some before you apply to the Army. After all, teamwork is an important aspect of the job.

Sample Response

"Yes, I have many years' experience of working in a team environment. To begin with, I have been playing hockey for my local team for the last three years. We worked really hard together improving our skills over the course of last season and we managed to win the league. I am also very much involved in teamwork in my current job. I work as a nurse at the local hospital and in order for the ward to function correctly we must work effectively as a team. My job is to check all of the patients at the beginning of my shift and also make sure that we have enough medical supplies to last the duration. It is then my

responsibility to inform the ward sister that the checks have been carried out. She will then obtain more supplies if we need them. We have to work very closely together for many hours and we all pull together whenever the going gets tough. I enjoy working in a team environment and feel comfortable whilst working under pressure."

Sample Question

Do you enjoy working in a team environment?

The best answer for this type of question is to state that you very much enjoy working in a team environment and that you are adaptable and can work in any role within a team. When answering this type of question try to give examples of situations where you have been an effective team member and achieved a common goal. The following sample response is better geared towards someone who has worked in an office environment prior to applying for the Army.

Sample Response

"In a previous role I was required to work as part of a 30-strong sales team. I really enjoyed the atmosphere within that team and managed to learn so much from other members. Yes I do enjoy working in a team environment but conversely my adaptability allows me to work in any environment. I would say that I can work either as one of a team or an individual depending on the requirements of the role. If I am required to work as part of a team then I will always listen carefully to the provided brief by my officer-in-command, keep in communication with the other team members, support those people who need supporting in the team, and also learn from any mistakes that the team makes so that we can improve next time.

I can remember one particular occasion when I was required to work as part of a team. Sales figures for the month were low and we were required to work as a team in order to generate new business leads. We all came together as a team and discussed the different options available to us. My role within the team was to source potential new clients over a two-week period whilst others sent out promotional materials once I had created the new leads. As a team we managed to increase sales and revenue by 50% in just a short space of time."

Sample Question

Give an example of when you have had to work as a team.

During your response to this question you MUST provide a specific situation where you have previously worked as a team. Take a look at the following sample response which will give you some good pointers for constructing your own.

Sample Response

"I have had lots of experience to date working as part of a team. In my current role as a bricklayer I have been working on a project with many other skilled workers and labourers. The project involves building ten new houses within a three-month period. We are now half way through the project and it is running smoothly and on time.

During this particular project I have been required to work with people who I did not know before the start of the build. This has not been a problem for me as I have no issue with working with anyone, regardless of who they are. I always start off by introducing myself to the rest of the team and ask the other team members to introduce themselves. This acts as a bit of an ice-breaker and it gets everyone talking. At the start of each working day we listen carefully to the brief provided by the foreman. As we work through the tasks set by the foreman we communicate with each other clearly so that everyone knows what is going on and whereabouts we all are with the project. If anyone in the building team starts to slow up we all gather round to help them catch up. As a team member I am always focused on the end goal and work very hard to carry out my job meticulously and diligently."

Sample Question

> **What would you do if a member of your team was not pulling their weight or doing their job effectively?**

This question is great preparation for Army Officer Entry, simply because the situation is something you may have to deal with in the future whilst managing your troops. Take a look at the following sample response to this question.

Sample Response

"I would first of all ask them if there was anything wrong, or if there was anything I could do to support them. The member of the team might be having personal issues, and if this was the case, I would want to support them and help them through it. If it was simply a case of them being lazy, then I would take immediate action to stop it. I would take them to one side and tactfully point out to them how important their role was within the team. I would inform them that without their full attention on the task in hand we would not be able to achieve our goal. I would also consider discipline procedures if appropriate and/or remedial training."

RESILIENCE

When preparing your responses to questions based on resilience I recommend you provide details about your physical fitness activity and also a demonstration of how capable you are at handling the pressures of serving in the Army. We have now provided a couple of questions to help you prepare.

Sample Question

> What have you done to prepare for life in the Army and tell me a bit about your fitness activity?

Sample Response

"I have been preparing for the selection process for a number of months now. To begin with I have been finding out about life within the Army and the types of challenges I will have to face, such as taking responsibility for myself and my actions and also coping with being away from home for long periods of time. To assist me in my preparation for life within the Army I have taken on lots of extra duties and responsibilities at home and around the house. For example, every day I clean one area of the house thoroughly and I am also responsible for ironing everyone's clothes in the household. This has been great practise for my training course, if I am to be successful.

With regards to my fitness I have been working very hard in this area. Although I am already a competent swimmer I have been going to my local pool four times a week and each time I swim 50 lengths of the 25 metre pool using a variety of different strokes. I have also been getting up at 6 a.m. each morning and running three miles each time, just to get used to the early starts.

I fully understand that life will be tough when I start the training course, but I am fully prepare for what lies ahead and I believe I have the maturity and responsibility to make sure I am successful and above all an asset to the Army team."

Sample Question

> Provide an example of where you have completed a task despite pressure from others. What did you do and what did you say?

Sample Response

"In my current job as car mechanic for a well-known company I was presented with a difficult and pressurised situation. A member

of the team had made a mistake and had fitted a number of wrong components to a car. The car in question was due to be picked up at 2 p.m. and the customer had stated how important it was that his car was ready on time because he had an important meeting to attend. We only had two hours in which to resolve the issue and I volunteered to be the one who would carry out the work on the car. The problem was that we had three other customers in the workshop waiting for their cars too, so I was the only person who could be spared at that particular time. In order to solve the problem I first of all gathered appropriate information. This included exactly what needed to be done and in what priority. I also established what realistically could be done and what couldn't be done in the timeframe given. I worked solidly for the next two hours making sure that I meticulously carried out each task in line with our operating procedures. Even though I didn't finish the car until 2.10pm, I managed to achieve all of the tasks under pressurised conditions whilst keeping strictly to procedures and regulations."

Sample Question

Provide an example of where you have had to make a difficult decision despite pressure from other people.

Sample Response

"My son is in his final year at the local school. To date, his work has been exceptional and every parents evening we attend he is praised by his teachers. However, recently there was an incident that involved very poor judgment on my son's part. He got involved with a group of youths from school who were bullying a boy who was less fortunate than themselves. The matter was brought to my attention by the boy's Father. He contacted me by letter and explained that my son had allegedly been involved in the bullying behaviour with the other youths. I immediately asked my son if the allegations were true. He immediately owned up to his part in the bullying, much to our disappointment. I decided that the best course of action was to take my son into school and to make the Head Teacher aware of the situation with a view to my son being punished in line with the school's disciplinary procedures. My wife totally disagreed with my

planned course of action and started to put pressure on me to deal with this within the family environment.

However, I maintained my stance. I was determined that my son should be punished by the school first and foremost. By taking this course of action I believed that my son would learn from his mistake and that he would never carry out this dreadful act again. I also wanted to ensure that the other offending youths were punished by the school too, as this would act as a deterrent to anyone else in the school who was thinking of bullying an individual.

Whilst my wife still disagreed with me to this day I believe the course of action I took was appropriate given the seriousness of the situation. My son was punished by the school and has since maintained a very high level of discipline both at school and at home."

Sample Question

How do you keep yourself fit and why do you think fitness is important to the role of someone serving in the Army?

Sample Response

"Yes, I keep myself fit and active and it is an important part of my life. I go swimming three times a week and swim 30 lengths every time I go. I go jogging twice a week to break up the routine and mix in some light weight work at the gym every now and again.

I also play football for my local Sunday team, which involves one practise session every fortnight. Plus I ensure that I eat a proper diet, which helps to keep me feeling confident and healthy.

Yes, I think that fitness is vital to the role of someone serving in the Army. The role involves working long hours and coupled with the fact that the work can be physically demanding, it is important that Army Officers and Soldiers stay fit and healthy so that they can perform to their peak and cope with the demands of the job."

PLANNING AND ORGANISING

Being able to plan and organise is all part and parcel of Army life. Make sure you can provide examples of when you have planned or organised an event. You should also be able to provide examples of how you keep your life organised and also provide details of what you do in your spare time. Make sure you use your spare time wisely and constructively!

Sample Question

> Provide an example of where you have taken personal responsibility to arrange or organise an event or situation.

Sample Response

"After reading an appeal in my local paper from a local charity, I decided to try to raise money for this worthwhile cause by organising a charity car wash day at the local school during the summer holidays. I decided that the event would take place in a month's time, which would give me enough time to organise such an event.

I set about organising the event and soon realised that I had made a mistake in trying to arrange everything on my own, so I arranged for two of my work colleagues to assist me. Once they had agreed to help I asked one of them to organise the booking of the school and arrange local sponsorship in the form of buckets, sponges and car wash soap to use on the day, so that we did not have to use our own personal money to buy them. I asked the second person to arrange advertising in the local newspaper and radio stations so that we could let the local community know about our charity car wash event, which would in turn hopefully bring in more money on the day for the charity.

Following a successful advertising campaign, I was inundated with calls from local newspapers about our event, and it was becoming hard work having to keep talking to them and explaining what the event was all about. But I knew that this information was important if we were to raise our target of £500.

Everything was going well right up to the morning of the event, when I realised we had not got the key to open the school gates. It was the summer holidays so the caretaker was not there to open the gates for us.

Not wanting to let everyone down, I jumped in my car and made my way down to the caretaker's house and managed to wake him up and get the key just in time before the car wash event was due to start. In the end the day was a great success and we all managed to raise £600 for the local charity."

Sample Question

Tell me what you get up to in your spare time or at weekends.

Sample Response

"I like to use my time wisely and I don't like sitting around doing nothing. More recently my time has been spent preparing for the selection process. Therefore, I have been getting up every day at 6 a.m. and going for a run before work. During lunchtime I have been reading my literature about the Army, Army Officer training and studying for this interview too. When I get home in the evenings I sometimes go swimming and then I will often go and play five-a-side football with my friends.

When it comes to the weekends I still keep fit and active by going on long and challenging walks, or going camping with friends. I am very much an active person who likes to make the most of the outdoors."

PROBLEM SOLVING

Taking personal responsibility to solve problems yourself is very much part of life within the Army, which is why you will probably be asked to provide an example of when you have solved a problem on your own or as part of a team.

Sample Question

Provide an example of where you have solved a difficult problem. What did you do?

Sample Response

"I was working in a retail shop and it was a busy trading day in the run up to Christmas. We had been advertising a promotion for a new brand of perfume in the local press that was due to launch the very next day. All of a sudden a member of staff approached me and informed me that no stock of the new perfume had been delivered and that time had run out to get any delivered before the following day's trade commenced. This obviously spelt disaster for the company as many people had placed pre-orders of the new perfume and they would be coming in to the store to collect their goods.

I started off by calling a meeting of three key members of staff. We gathered in the staff room and I coordinated a brain storming session in order to resolve the issue. I started off by gathering as much information as possible. The key facts I gained were:

1. *The amount of time we had left in order to get some stock delivered.*

2. *How much stock we needed to fulfil pre-orders.*

3. *Who was available to work late that evening?*

4. *Who had transport and a full driving licence?*

Once I had gathered the facts I then developed a plan to resolve the problem. I asked a member of the team to phone around all company stores in the county to establish which shops had extra stock. I then assigned another member of staff who was willing to work late to drive out to the stores in order to borrow the extra surplus stock. I then personally placed an initial order with the distributer so that we had enough stock to fulfil orders for the entire Christmas period and to also pay back the stock we had borrowed from other stores in the County.

The result of the situation was that we managed to obtain sufficient stock to fulfil the orders the next day. Finally, I carried out a full investigation as to why this situation had occurred in the first place with a view to making sure it never happened again."

Sample Question

Provide an example of where you have solved a problem in a work situation?

Sample Response

"I was working at a restaurant and noticed a divide between the waiters and kitchen staff. This was a problem that had to be resolved as it was impacting on the effectiveness of the team. Most of the kitchen staff were older than their waiter colleagues and had migrated from India. There was very little interaction between the kitchen and waiter staff colleagues and I was concerned that this barrier would not only make the kitchen staff feel isolated, but that it would also have a negative impact on the team environment.

My initial considerations were to ensure that the kitchen staff felt comfortable and that they could speak to me and the waiters if they needed help or assistance. After all, they had not been in the country for long and I wanted them to feel welcome and valued. I believe that communication between colleagues within a workplace is essential to achieve the best possible results and create a good working environment, regardless of individual differences.

To overcome the challenges I introduced myself to all the kitchen staff members and I learnt their names. This ensured that they felt valued, and that they also had a point of contact if they ever needed assistance or support. I also encouraged the other waiters to communicate with their kitchen colleagues. Following my actions communication improved and the workplace is now a more efficient and happier working environment."

LEARNING AND DEVELOPING

Continuous development during your career in the Army is very important. Therefore, during the interview you will probably be asked to provide details of an occasion on which you have learnt a new skill, or improved an existing one.

Sample Question

Tell me about a time when you have taken it upon yourself to learn a new skill or develop an existing one?

How to structure your response:

- What skill did you learn or develop?

- What prompted this development?

- When did this learning or development occur or take place?

- How did you go about learning or developing this skill?

- What was the result?

- How has this skill helped you since then?

Sample Response

"Although I am in my late twenties I had always wanted to learn to play the guitar. It is something that I have wanted to do for many years, but have never had the time to learn until recently. One day I was watching a band play with my wife at my local pub and decided there and then that I would make it my mission to learn to play competently. The following day I went onto the Internet and searched for a good guitar tutor in my local area. Luckily, I managed to find one within my town who had a very good reputation for teaching. I immediately booked a block of lessons and started my first one within a week. My development in the use of playing the guitar progressed rapidly and I soon achieved grade one standard. Every night of the week I would dedicate at least 30 minutes of time to my learning, in addition to my one hour weekly lesson. I soon found that I was progressing through the grades quickly, which was due to my level of learning commitment and a desire to become competent in playing the instrument.

I recently achieved grade four and I am now working to grade five standard. I am also now playing in a local band, and the opportunities for me, both musically and socially, have increased tenfold since learning to play. In addition to this, learning to play the guitar has improved my concentration levels and my patience."

Sample Question

Tell me about a time when you changed how you did something in response to feedback from someone else.

Sample Response

"During my last appraisal, my line manager identified that I needed to improve in a specific area. I work as a call handler for a large independent communications company. Part of my role involves answering a specific number of calls per hour. If I do not reach my target then this does not allow the company to meet its standards. I found that I was falling behind on the number of calls answered and this was identified during the appraisal. I needed to develop my skills in the manner in which I handled the call. My line manager played back a number of recorded calls that I had dealt with and

it was apparent that I was taking too long speaking to the customer about issues that were irrelevant to the call itself. Because I am a conscientious and caring person I found myself asking the customer how they were and what kind of day they were having. I was spending too much time on delivering a high quality service to the customer, as opposed to working through the call as fast as possible so that I could answer the next one.

Despite the customers being more than pleased with level of customer care, this approach was not helping the company and therefore I needed to change my approach. I immediately took on-board the comments of my line manager and also took up the offer of development and call handling training. After the training, which took two weeks to complete, I was meeting my targets with ease. This in turn helped the company to reach its call handling targets."

DISCIPLINE

You don't need me to tell you how important discipline is in a career such as the Army, but how you answer the questions based around this competency is very important. You need to be able to demonstrate that you can take instructions from people in senior positions, and also demonstrate how self-disciplined you are either at home, in education or in a work setting. Before you attend the Army Officer interview be able to provide answers to questions like these. Here is a sample question and answer to help you prepare.

Sample Question

> Can you give an example when you have followed instructions or guidelines in order to complete a task?

Sample Response

"Whilst working in my current role as a gas engineer I was tasked with fitting a new boiler to a domestic property. I carried out this work unsupervised and was relied upon to follow strict procedural and safety guidelines. If I did not follow the procedural guidance that I received during my training then I would be putting lives at risk. I must ensure that I carry out my work responsibly and follow all safety procedures to ensure that my work is carried out in accordance with my company's policies. The boiler was fitted to the required standard in accordance with the relevant British Standard and all safety procedures were followed. The customer was satisfied with my work and I was happy that I carried out my duties responsibly. I fully understand the importance of being self-disciplined in the Army, and if you do not follow rules and procedures or follow instructions then this can endanger people's lives and also jeopardise a mission."

Sample Question

> **Tell me about your educational exam results. Were you satisfied with them and what did you think of your teachers and your school?**

This question is designed to see what you personally think about your results, and also your attitude to your education and to people (your teachers) who are in positions of authority. If you didn't get the results that you wanted then just say so. However, it is important to tell the interviewer what you plan to do about them and what your plans are for the future. When I passed Armed Forces selection many years ago I had a six month wait before I could start my basic training. The Warrant Officer at the AFCO advised that I embarked on an educational foundation course at college for the six month period whilst I waited to commence my basic training. I took his advice and I am glad that I did.

Because you are applying to become an Officer then you will obviously have already met the minimum qualification requirements for the role; however, you should consider whether or not you could have achieved improved scores if you had applied yourself more effectively during your educational years.

The second part of the question is very important. Questions of this nature are designed to see how you react to discipline. Many of us probably did not get on with at least one of our teachers during our educational years; however, keep your personal opinions of your teachers to yourself and focus on displaying your ability to respect and understand the need for discipline.

Sample Response

"I achieved high standards on the majority of exams, but I wasn't satisfied with my Math's result. I know I could have done better. Since my results I've been working hard to improve my skills in this area and I have embarked on an evening course which will gain me a better grade. I am a determined person and I'm always looking to improve my skills. One of my strengths is that I can see what I need to work on and I always make sure I work hard to make the necessary improvements. In relation to my teachers and my school I have a lot of respect for them. The teachers are in positions of authority and it is

important to respect that. I also understand that if I am successful in my pursuit to join the Army it will be very important to be disciplined at all times. Whilst I will be leading a team once qualified and out of training I also understand that I will need to act as a positive role model for the men and women under my Command. Discipline is at the core of all operations and without it things can go wrong and tasks and objectives may not be met. I can be relied upon to maintain and encourage positive discipline at all times during my Army career."

COMMUNUCATION SKILLS

During the interview the interviewer will be looking to see how you communicate, and also how you structure your responses to the interview questions. Consider the following points both during the interview and whilst responding to the interview questions:

- When you walk into the interview room stand up straight and introduce yourself. Be polite and courteous at all times and try to come across in a pleasant manner. The panel will be assessing you as soon as you walk through the door so make sure you make a positive first impression.

- Do not sit down in the interview chair until you are invited to do so. This is good manners.

- When you sit down in the interview chair, sit up straight and do not fidget or slouch. It is acceptable to use hand gestures when explaining your responses to the questions but don't overdo it, as they can become a distraction.

- Structure your responses to the questions in a logical manner – this is very important. When responding to an interview question, start at the beginning and work your way through in a concise manner, and at a pace that is easy for the panel to listen to.

- Speak clearly and in a tone that is easy for the panel to hear. Be confident in your responses.

- When talking to the panel use eye contact but be careful not to look at them in an intimidating manner.

- Wear a formal outfit to the interview such as a suit. You are applying to join the Armed Forces, which is a disciplined environment.

Therefore, you need to demonstrate that you are capable of dressing smartly and also taking pride in your appearance.

FINAL GOLDEN INTERVIEW TIPS

- Always provide 'specific' examples to the questions being asked that are based around competencies.

- During your responses try to outline your contributions and also provide evidence of the competency area that is being assessed.

- Speak clearly, use correct English and structure your responses in a logical and concise manner.

Now let's take a look at a number of generic sample interview questions. Please note that these questions are not guaranteed to be the exact ones you'll come up against at the real interview, but they are good starting point in your preparation.

Use the sample responses that I have provided as a basis for your own preparation. Construct your answers on your own opinions and experiences.

CHAPTER 2

GENERIC QUESTIONS FOR THE INTERVIEW

Question 1

Why do you want to join the Army?

This is an almost guaranteed question during your Army interview so there should be no reason why you can't answer it in a positive manner. Try to display motivation when answering questions of this nature. The Army are looking for people who want to become a professional member of their team and who understand the Army way of life. By studying your Army recruitment literature and the Army website you will understand what service life is all about. You want to be a member of the British Army and you are attracted to what it has to offer. If you have been pushed into joining by your family then you shouldn't be applying.

Sample Response

"I have wanted to join the Army for a number of years now and feel that I have now reached a part of my life where I am ready to commit to the service. Having studied the Army recruitment literature and visited the Army website, I am impressed by the professionalism and standards the service sets itself.

I would like a career that is fulfilling, challenging and rewarding and I believe that the Army would provide all of these. I enjoy keeping physically fit and active and believe that given the right training I would make a great team member. I am also very much attracted to the fact that the Army offers a wide choice of careers for the role of Officer.

The fact that I would be improving my education and managing men and women is just another example of why I want to join the service. I have seriously considered the implications that joining a service such as the Army would have on both my personal life and social life and discussed these with my family. They have given me their full support and commitment in helping me to achieve my goal of joining the Army as an Officer."

Question 2

What does your family think of you wanting to join the Army?

Again, you are likely to be asked a question surrounding your family background and what they think about you wanting to join the Army. It is important that your family support you in your decision.

If they have any doubts about you joining the service then you may wish to consider taking them along to the AFCO so they can ask any questions or raise any concerns that they may have. When answering questions such as this it is important that you are honest and tell the truth. If your family have any concerns then share them with the careers officer, who will then be able to advise you on the best way for your family/partner to overcome any fears they may have.

Sample Response

"I have discussed the issue with them in depth and also shown them all of the Army recruitment literature to try to dampen any fears that they may have.

They were initially apprehensive about me joining but they gave me their full support after I told them everything I know about the training I will go through and the conditions I will serve under, if I am successful in my pursuit to join as an Officer. They are aware that the Army has a good reputation and this has helped them to further understand why I want to join. They have seen how enthusiastic I am about wanting to join the Army and know that it will be great for me. I have also discussed the issue with my partner and he/she is extremely supportive. They are all looking forward to hopefully seeing me at my passing out parade at Sandhurst and therefore I have their full backing."

Question 3

How do you think you will cope with Army life in relation to the discipline and being part of a military organisation?

When you join the Army you will be joining a military organisation that has set procedures, standards and discipline codes. To some people this will come as a shock and the Army want to know that you are prepared for this change in lifestyle. It is even more important when you join as an Officer as you will need to act as a role model to the people under your Command. The Army is investing time, effort and resources into your training so they want to know that you can cope with their way of life.

When answering this type of question you need to demonstrate both your awareness of what Army life involves, your positive attitude towards the disciplined environment and also your understanding of the need to lead by example. Study the recruitment literature and visit the Army website to get a feel for the type of training you will be going through.

Sample Response

"Having read the information available to me about the Army way of life I think I would cope very well. I know that I will find it difficult at times but believe I have both the maturity and stability to succeed and become a competent member of the team. I am also fully aware of the need to lead by example and act as a positive role model to those whom will be under my Command as an officer. The very nature of the Army means that it requires a disciplined workforce. Without that discipline things can go wrong. If the men and women under my Command do not carry out their duties professionally then they could endanger somebody's life. I understand why discipline is required and believe I would cope with it well. I understand that being in the Army isn't a 9-5 job, but instead you must take on tasks whenever required.

In order to prepare for the training I have already integrated routine and self-discipline into my life. For example, I have been getting up at 6am every weekday morning to go running and I have started carrying out daily household tasks such as hovering, cleaning and ironing.

At the start of my preparation for joining the Army I made myself an action plan that would focus my mind on what I needed to do in order to improve."

Question 4

How do you think you will cope with being away from home and losing your personal freedom?

This type of question is one that needs to be answered positively. There is only one correct answer to this question and you need to demonstrate that you have considered the consequences of leaving home and are fully aware of what is involved. If you have any experience of being away from home then you should state this in your response. Try to think of occasions when you have been away for periods of time and tell them that it wasn't an issue.

Have you ever been a part of any youth organisations? If you have then this will undoubtedly go in your favour. Giving an example is far better than just saying you will be able to cope.

Sample Response

"Having already had experience of being away from home, I believe I would cope extremely well. Whilst serving with the Army Cadets a few years ago I was introduced to the Army way of life and fully understand what it is like to be away from home. I actually enjoy being away from home and I can't wait to get started if I am successful during selection. I understand however that the training is difficult and intense and I am fully prepared for this. I am confident that I will cope with the change in lifestyle very well and I am looking forward to the challenge if I am accepted."

Question 5

Are you involved in any sporting activities and how do you keep yourself fit?

When answering questions based around your own physical fitness you need to be honest but bear in mind the following points:

Although you don't have to be super fit to join the Army, you do need to have a good level of physical fitness, so being fit in the first instance is an obvious advantage. The Army, just like the other Armed Forces, pride themselves on their ability to work as an effective team unit. Those people who engage in active team sports are more likely to be competent team members. If you play a team sport then this will be a good thing to tell them. If you don't then it may be a good idea to go and join one! Regardless of the above points, remember that if you don't do any physical activity whatsoever then you will score low in this area. Make sure you partake in some form of physical activity. During the ADSC you will be required to carry out a 1.5 mile run which should be your 'best effort'.

The Army has realised that those people who cannot complete the run in less than 14 minutes are far more likely to suffer from injury during the initial training course. Start running now so that you can easily pass the forthcoming physical tests.

Sample Response

"Yes I am. I currently play in the local hockey team and have been doing that for a number of years now. Maintaining a good level of fitness is something I enjoy. In fact, recently I have increased my fitness levels by going swimming three times a week. I'm aware that during the recruit training course I will be pushed to my limits so I need to be prepared for that. I believe the fact that I play team sports will help me get through my training.

I enjoy playing in a hockey team because when we are being beaten by another team everyone always pulls together and we work hard to try to win the game back. After the game we all meet in the club bar for a drink and chat about the game. Keeping fit is important to me and something that I want to continue doing throughout my career if I am successful in joining the Army."

Question 6

What responsibilities do you have either at work, school or at home?

When you join the Army as an Officer you will need to take full responsibility for yourself, your team, your equipment and also for the safety of your work colleagues. At the age of eighteen I was responsible for servicing and maintaining Sea Harrier jets on board HMS Invincible. I was responsible for going out on deck at 4 a.m. and servicing the ejector seats that formed part of the pilot's safety equipment. That was a huge responsibility to undertake at such a young age. Before you join the Army as an Officer you will need to demonstrate that you can handle responsibility. The most effective way to do this is by providing the interviewer with examples of where you have already held positions of responsibility either at home, work or during your education.

Sample Response

"I currently hold a large number of responsibilities both at home and in my part-time job. I am responsible for cleaning the house top to bottom once a week and I usually do this on a Sunday before I go and play football for my local team. I'm also captain of the football team which means I have to arrange the fixtures, book the football ground and I also collect the kit at the end of the match and get it washed and dried for the following week's fixture. I also take control of the clubs financial affairs as I have an interest in accountancy. I thoroughly enjoy this responsibility and would not have it any other way; I am always the first to volunteer for any task or role that involves a level of responsibility. In addition to this I have just started a new part-time job at my local supermarket as a junior supervisor. This involves managing five members of staff, managing stock levels and also managing resources.

It is essential that I make sure the store has sufficient resources to operate effectively every day that it is open.

I enjoy taking on responsibility as it gives me a sense of achievement. I understand that I will need to be responsible during my Initial Officer Training not only for myself, but also for ensuring that I work hard to pass every assessment in order to develop into a competent member of the Army establishment."

Question 7

What do you think the qualities of a good team player are?

I have already made reference to the importance of teamwork during this guide and there is a possibility that you will be asked a question that relates to your ability to work as part of a team and also what you think the qualities of an effective team worker are. Whilst on missions and training exercises with the Army there is a high risk that things can go wrong.

If something serious goes wrong then you have to work very fast and professionally as part of a team in order to resolve the issue. Before you can work effectively as a team however you need to know what the main qualities of a competent team member include. Take a look at the following:

- An ability to interact and work with others, regardless of their age, sex, religion, sexual orientation, background, disability or appearance;

- Being able to communicate with everyone in the team and provide the appropriate level of support and encouragement;

- Being capable of carrying out tasks correctly, professionally and in accordance with guidelines and regulations;

- Being focused on the team's goal(s);

- Having a flexible attitude and approach to the task;

- Putting the needs of the team first before your own;

- Putting personal differences aside for the sake of the team;

- Being able to listen to others' suggestions and contributions.

When responding to this type of question it would be an advantage if you could back up your response with an example in which you already work in a team.

Sample Response

"A good team player must have many different qualities including an ability to listen carefully to a given brief. If you don't listen to the brief that is provided then you can't complete the task properly. In addition to listening carefully to the brief you must be able to communicate effectively with everyone in the team. As an Army Officer this will be even more important. As a team member and leader I will be responsible for supporting the other team members and also listening to other people's suggestions about how a task can be achieved. You also have to be able to work with anyone in the team regardless of their age, background, religion, sexual orientation, disability or appearance. You can't discriminate against anyone and if you do, then there is no place for you within that team. A good team player must also be able to carry out his or her job professionally and competently. When I say competently I mean correctly and in accordance with guidelines and training. You should also be focused on the team's goal and not be distracted by any external factors. Putting the needs of the team first is paramount. Finally a good team player must be flexible and be able to adapt to the changing requirements of the team.

I already have some experience of working in a team and I know how important it is to work hard at achieving the task. I have a job working in my local supermarket as a junior supervisor and every week we have a team briefing. During the team briefings it is my responsibility to inform the team what tasks need to be carried out as a priority. During one particular meeting I asked the team to clear a fire escape that had become blocked with cardboard boxes, debris and rubbish. In addition to this I also asked the team to come up with a plan to prevent it from happening again. Once I had briefed the team members we all set about the task carefully removing the rubbish. Once this was completed we then worked together in order to devise a plan to prevent it from happening again. Whilst it is important to delegate work as a leader, it is just as important to be able to work as part of that team, encouraging, supporting and communicating as you progress through the task."

Question 8

What do you do in your spare time?

With questions of this nature the Army recruitment staff are looking to see if you use your leisure time wisely. Your response will tell them a lot about your attitude and motivation. We all know that some people spend their spare time doing nothing or watching TV and playing computer games. When you join the Army you won't have much time to sit around and do nothing. The Army will want to hear that you are active and doing worthwhile things during your spare time. For example, if you are involved in any sports, outdoor activities or are part of any youth organisation such as the Army Cadets then these are good things to tell them. You may also be involved in voluntary work or charity work and once again these will work in your favour if mentioned at interview.

If you currently do very little with your spare time then now is a good time to make a lifestyle change. Embark on a fitness routine or join an activity club or organisation.

Sample Response

"During my spare time I like to keep active, both physically and mentally. I enjoy visiting the gym three times a week and I have a structured workout that I try to vary every three months to keep my interest levels up. I'm also currently doing a part-time study course in Art, which is one of my hobbies. I'm also a member of the local Army Cadets, which is an evening's commitment every week and the occasional weekend.

Of course, I know when it is time to relax and usually do this by either listening to music or playing snooker with my friends, but overall I'm quite an active person. I certainly don't like sitting around doing nothing. I understand that if I'm successful at joining the Army there will be plenty of things to do in the evenings to keep me occupied such as the gym and other various social events."

Question 9

Can you tell us about any personal achievements you have experienced during your life so far?

Having achieved something in your life demonstrates that you have the ability to see things through to the end. It also shows that you are motivated and determined to succeed. The Army wants to see evidence that you can achieve, as there is a greater chance of you completing the initial recruit course if you have a history of this. Try to think of examples where you have succeeded or achieved something relevant in your life. Some good examples of achievements are as follows:

- Duke of Edinburgh's Award;

- A-levels or educational qualifications;

- Team or individual sports awards/trophies/medals;

- Raising money for charity.

Sample Response

"So far in my life I have managed to achieve a number of things that I am proud of. To begin with, I recently worked hard to achieve my 'GCSE' results, which enabled me to go on to further education and study my choice of subject. Without these grades I would not have been able to do that.

About a year ago the football team that I play in won the league trophy for the second year running, which is another one of my more recent achievements.

However, my most memorable achievement to date is managing to raise £1,000 for a local charity. I worked hard and ran a marathon in order to raise the money. I was particularly proud of this achievement because It meant the charity I ran for were able to purchase some important items of equipment that could be used to treat some of their patients."

Question 10

What are your strengths and what are you good at?

This is a common interview question that is relatively easy to answer. The problem with it is that many people use the same response. It is quite an easy thing to tell the interviewer that you are dedicated and the right person for the job. However, it is a different thing backing it up with evidence!

If you are asked this type of question make sure you are positive during your response and show that you actually mean what you are saying. Then, back up the strengths you have mentioned with specific examples which demonstrate the quality you are claiming to possess. For example, if you tell the panel that you are a motivated person, back it up with an example in your life where you have achieved something through sheer motivation and determination.

Sample Response

"To begin with, I'm a determined person who likes to see things through to the end. For example, I recently ran a marathon for charity. I'd never done this kind of thing before and found it very hard work, but I made sure I completed the task. Another strength of mine is that I'm always looking for ways to improve myself. As an example, I have been preparing for the Army Officer selection process by embarking on an evening class that will see me eventually achieve a Diploma in Management Studies. Although I have a small amount of managerial and supervisory experience, I want to make sure that I am in the best position possible for becoming a competent Army Officer. Finally, I would say that one of my biggest strengths is that I'm a great team player. I really enjoy working in a team environment and achieving things through a collaborative approach. For example, I play in a local rugby team and we recently won the league trophy for the first time since the club was established some 50 years ago."

Question 11

What are your weaknesses?

Now this is a difficult question to answer! We all have weaknesses and anyone who says they haven't, is probably not telling truth. However, you must be very careful how you respond to this question. Apart from being truthful you must also provide a weakness that you are working hard on to improve. You should also remember that you are joining a disciplined service that requires hard work, determination and a will to succeed. So, if you are the type of person who cannot get up in the morning and you keep making regular mistakes at work or at school, then the Army might not be for you.

The key to responding to this type of question is to be truthful but to also back it up with examples of what you are doing to improve your weakness.

Sample Response

"My biggest is weakness is that sometimes I work too hard. Once I get in from my day job I am straight upstairs working on my computer, studying for a course I have undertaken. Whilst being hard working is a positive aspect of my character, I do need to learn to relax and take time out. I will never be a lazy person and I really do get a lot out of working, but I must take more time to relax as this will help me to perform better when I am at work."

Question 12

Why do you want to become an Officer? Why don't you become a Rating instead? (Officer Applicant)

This type of question is designed to see if there are any genuine reasons why you have chosen to become an Officer. Some applicants get carried away with the perceived glamour and status of the role, without putting any serious thought into why they actually want to become an Officer. When preparing your response to this question you need to think about the skills and attributes that you have already gained that are relevant to the role of a Army Officer. You may already have some genuine reasons why you want to become an Officer but please read the following sample response which will give you some good pointers when preparing your response.

<u>Sample Response</u>

"I have thought long and hard about applying to become an Officer and I am fully certain that this is what I want to do. To begin with, I spent considerable time assessing my own qualities and attributes and I believe they would be most suited to that of an Officer. I am hard working, tenacious, resolute, professional, driven and ambitious and feel that these qualities will allow me to eventually become a competent Officer in the Army. In addition to my qualities I have already gained some experience in a supervisory role within my current job. I really enjoy the additional responsibility that this brings and would not thrive in a role that holds little or no responsibility. It is my ultimate goal to join the Army and serve as an Officer. I am determined and resolute and believe that I would make an invaluable contribution to this elite service."

Question 13

What are the values of the British Army?

During one of the very first stages of this guide I made reference to the Army values. Every soldier and officer is expected to abide by these important values and therefore it is not unreasonable for the Army to expect you to know them when you apply. You are likely to be asked a question that relates to the values during the ADSC so make sure you know them and what each one of them means.

Sample Response

"The values of the British Army are a selfless commitment, courage, discipline, integrity, loyalty and respect for others. As a soldier you have to be prepared to carry out tasks that others don't have to. It is important to be strong and aggressive in battle but to also behave properly and demonstrate self-control at all times. Army soldiers and officers have to be aggressive and strong in battle, yet behave properly and show self-control all of the time. Being courageous means facing up to danger and doing what is right at all times. Discipline means having the ability to maintain constant high standards, so that others can rely on you. Integrity means earning the respect and trust of your work colleagues. Loyalty is being faithful to your work colleagues and to your duty and having respect for others means treating everybody with respect and dignity at all times."

FURTHER SAMPLE INTERVIEW QUESTIONS

Q14.

Tell me about the basic training you will undergo as an Officer? (NOTE: When applying for Officer Entry it is advisable that you have knowledge of the Soldier's selection training too; after all, if you are managing Soldiers as an Officer then you should have knowledge of the type of training they will undergo!

Q15.

What is the minimum service contract you will be required to sign as an Officer or a Soldier?

Q16.

Which part of your training do you think you would find the hardest and what have you done to prepare for this?

Q17.

What have you been doing so far to prepare for the Army Officer Selection Board?

Q18.

If you fail Officer Selection, would you consider joining as a Soldier?

FINAL INTERVIEW TIPS

Within this section of the guide I will provide you with some final tips that will help you prepare for the filter interview. Remember that your success will very much depend on how prepared you are. Don't forget to work on your interview technique, carry out plenty of research and work on your responses to the interview questions.

- In the build-up to the interview carry out plenty of targeted preparation work. Read your recruitment literature and spend time studying the Army website. Ask the AFCO recruitment advisor to provide you with further information about the training you'll undergo. If you get the opportunity, speak to serving members of the Army to find out as much as possible about life within the Service.

- Work on your interview technique and make sure you try out at least one 'mock interview'. This involves getting your family or friends to sit you down and ask you the interview questions that are contained within this guide.

- When you receive your date for the interview make sure you turn up on time. Check your travel and parking arrangements the day before your interview. The last thing you need is to be late for your interview!

- Think carefully about what you are going to wear during the interview. I am not saying that you should go out and buy an expensive suit but I do recommend you make every effort to dress smartly and formally. Having said that, if you do decide to wear a smart suit or formal outfit, make sure it is clean and pressed. You can still look scruffy in a suit.

- Personal hygiene is all part and parcel of Army life. Don't attend the interview unwashed, dirty or fresh from the building site!

- When you walk into the interview room, stand up straight with your shoulders back. Project an image of confidence and be polite, courteous and respectful to the interviewer at all times.

- Don't sit down in the interview chair until invited to do so. This will display good manners.

- Whilst you are in the interview chair sit upright with your hands resting on your knees, palms facing downwards. It is acceptable to use your hands expressively, but don't overdo it.

- Don't slouch in the chair. At the end of each question readjust your position.

- Whilst responding to the interview questions make sure you speak up and be positive. You will need to demonstrate a level of motivation and enthusiasm during the interview.

- Go the extra mile and learn a little bit about the Army's history. When the panel asks you "what can you tell us about the Army?" you will be able to demonstrate that you have made an effort to look into their history as well as their modern day activities.

- Ask positive questions at the end of the interview. Don't ask questions such as "How much leave will I get?" or "How often do I get paid?"

- If you are unsure about a question do not to 'waffle'. If you do not know the answer, then it is acceptable to say so. Move on to the next question and put it behind you. Remember, you are being assessed against your communication skills, so a bit of preparation in this area will not go a miss!

- Finally, believe in yourself and be confident.

CHAPTER 3
THE ARMY OFFICER SELECTION BOARD

Before I go on to explain the scoring criteria, let us first of all take a look at some additional competencies required to successfully pass the Army Officer initial training course at Sandhurst. Having an understanding of these will help you prepare better for the interview.

COMPETENCIES REQUIRED FOR SUCCESS DURING INITIAL OFFICER TRAINING

Interpersonal Competencies

Communicating effectively	Is able to communicate accurately and effectively both orally and in writing.
Teamwork	Is able to work with others to achieve common goals.
Influencing	Can influence others to follow a certain course of action.

Problem Solving Competencies

Appreciation	Comprehends, identifies, extracts and assimilates information from a range of sources, quickly and accurately.
Reasoning	Thinks logically, practically and coherently to produce a successful or reasonable solution, quickly and accurately.
Organisation	Determines priorities and allocates resources effectively and efficiently to a task(s).
Capacity	Holds and processes multiple inputs whilst maintaining task performance.

Character Competencies

Decisiveness	Makes sound appropriate decisions within timescale demanded by the situation.
Self-motivation	Demonstrates a high level of commitment and interest to tasks.
Self-analysis	Monitors and objectively analyses own performance.
Integrity	Behaviour is guided by principles, morals and ethics appropriate to service life. Adheres to rules and regulations specific to the Army.

Now that we understand some of the competencies that are required to pass Initial Officer Training, we can explore the type of qualities the assessors will be looking for during the Army Officer Selection Board.

EXAMPLES OF COMPETENCIES ASSESSED DURING THE AOSB

Example competency	Description
Communication	• Delivers communication in a concise and effective manner, both written and orally. • Listens to others' suggestions. • Contributes when appropriate. • Understands the situation/discussion.
Teamwork	• Is able to work with others in order to achieve a task or goal. • Puts in plenty of effort. • Treats others appropriately. • Supports other team members. • Communicates with the team. • Encourages the team.
Influencing	• Has considerable impact on others. • Can persuade and direct others.
Problem Solving	• Can judge certain situations. • Is flexible. • Is decisive. • Can come up with solutions to most problems.
Confidence and Resilience	• Self-assured. • Is composed and calm. • Perseveres. • Determined. • Resolute.

WHEN ARE THE COMPETENCIES ASSESSED?

Each of the qualities will be assessed during every stage of the AOSB, although some more than others. For example, you will be assessed on your influencing capabilities considerably during the planning exercise and your teamwork skills during the Command Tasks. For the interviews which form part of the AOSB, you should concentrate on demonstrating ability and competence in every single area!

CHAPTER 4
HOW TO PASS
THE INTERVIEW

During this section of the guide I will provide you with a number of sample interview questions and advice on how to answer them. Whilst some of the questions will appear to be easy to answer, it is still important that we cover them, in order to ensure that you are fully prepared for you AOSB. You will find that some of the questions in this section are duplicated. The reason for this is simply because some people who use this book will only be interested in the AOSB section having already passed their initial filter interview(s).

I have divided the sample questions into various different sections to assist you during your preparation.

PERSONAL QUESTIONS

Questions that are based on your personal details are obviously very easy to answer. However, you need to ensure that your responses demonstrate you have the key skills and attributes to carry out the role of an Officer. After some of the questions I will provide tips on how I believe you should answer them.

Q. Where are you living now and who are you living with?

Whilst it is acceptable for you to still live with your parents, the assessor may be looking for a level of independence here. If you do live with your parents then state that this has been a temporary measure whilst you prepare for Army Officer selection. Tell the interviewer that you are fully independent at home and that you have lots of responsibilities, such as ironing, cleaning and also some financial responsibilities too.

Q. Where else have you lived apart from with your parents?

Again, aim to demonstrate a level of independence. If you have lived with other people during your early life then it may be easier for you to adapt to life during training, on exercise and whilst serving in the Army in general.

Q. Describe your home life to me.

I am certainly not telling you what to say here; however, if it was me answering this question I would be looking to tell the interviewer that my home life was stable yet disciplined. I would also inform them that I had plenty of responsibilities whilst at home, including cleaning, ironing and also financial responsibilities. Having said that, it is absolutely fine to tell the panel if your home life was unsettled – what is important is what you have learnt from your experiences and how they have helped you to prepare for Army life as an Officer.

Q. What was your life like growing up?

Questions that relate to your home life are designed to assess how stable you are as person, whether or not you have any responsibilities at home, whether you are generally a happy person and also what you have learnt from life's experiences to date.

Things to consider:

- Know key dates of where you have lived.

- Try and provide examples of where you have moved around. This demonstrates that you are flexible and adaptable when the need arises.

- The more responsibilities you have at home, such as washing, ironing, cleaning, financial responsibilities etc, the better.

- If you have lived with other people, apart from your immediate family, tell them so. Remember – as an Army Officer you will be living with men and women of different ages etc.

EDUCATION

Q. How many schools have you attended and what years did you attend them?

Q. What did you think about your teachers?

Do not, under any circumstances, be disrespectful about your teachers when answering this question – if you do, the chances of passing AOSB will be slim! Remember that you are applying to join a disciplined service and therefore, it is crucial that you demonstrate respect for people in positions of authority, regardless of whether you liked them or not!

Q. Tell me about your exam results; did you achieve the grades you wanted?

Q. Could you have worked harder whilst at school?

Although these are relatively easy questions to respond to, ones that relate to your exam results and how hard you worked whilst at school could catch you out. You have to be honest about your results. If they were not up to the standard that you expected, have a valid reason why. Never be disrespectful of your teachers or the educational system. Remember that you are applying to join a disciplined service.

SCHOOL / COLLEGE

Q. Did you learn anything from other students?

During the first section of this interview guide I provided you with sample responses to questions based around 'learning and developing'. This question gauges whether or not you have the ability to learn from others. Regardless of who we are or how old we are, we can ALL learn from others. My advice would be to think of a situation you have been in where you have learnt from other people, either in an educational-based scenario or work-based one.

Q. Did you have any responsibilities whilst at school or college?

Because you are applying to become an Officer then it is important you demonstrate previous experience of having assumed responsibility or leadership of a project or other people. Good examples to use here would be if you were the captain of a football or hockey team, or even Head of Year!

Q. What sports did you participate in whilst at school or college?

If you didn't participate in any sports at school then you need to have a good reason why not! Being active and playing team sports is not only great for your physical and mental fitness, but it is also essential for your leadership and team working capabilities. When talking at interview about the sports you are or have been involved in, talk with a level of enthusiasm and also talk about any trophies or competitions you won. Being an 'achiever' is something the panel will want to see here as it will demonstrate to them that you have the ability to complete tasks to a high standard.

Q. What clubs or societies were you a member of?

Q. Do you have the Duke of Edinburgh or similar awards?

Being a member of a team or society is a positive thing, simply because being in the Army is very much like being part of a winning team! Try and give positive examples of teams, clubs or organisations you have been a part of during your life.

Q. Where did you travel to with school?

Previous experience of travelling with other people is good, simply because that's what you will be doing when you join the Army.

Q. Did you have any gaps in your education?

If you did have any gaps in your education, it is better to say that you used the time wisely. Maybe you went travelling around the world in order to gain new experiences and cultures, or maybe you wanted to take time out from your studies to take on a work related role or even a charity role. Whatever you do, do not say that you did nothing with your time off. If you went travelling, what did you gain from the experience?

Whilst at school or college it would be an advantage if you had some level of responsibility. For example, maybe you were a prefect or head of year, or maybe you were the captain of a sports team. You are applying to become an Officer, which effectively means you are going to be a manager and a leader. Having some previous experience of these important roles will be an advantage. If you haven't had any responsibilities in your life to date, how do you know that you'll be a good leader or manager in the Army?

OUTSIDE INTERESTS AND HOBBIES

When responding to questions based on your interests and hobbies I recommend that you provide ones that demonstrate you are both active and a team player. Interests that also demonstrate your ability to learn new skills are also positive attributes to mention.

Q. What sports are you currently engaged in?

Try and provide sports that involve teamwork, such as:

- Rugby;
- Hockey;
- Football;
- Netball.

I also advise that you become a competent swimmer prior to applying to join the Army, if you are not already.

Q. What sporting achievements have you gained?

If you can provide any proof of sporting achievements, either as part of a team or individually, then great! The panel will want to see evidence of achievements you have gained to date, as this will provide reassurance that you are more likely to complete the tough recruitment course. Demonstrating a history of achievement is very important when applying to join the Army.

Q. Have you been part of any youth organisations such as the Scouts, Army Cadets, Guides or Sea Cadets etc?

Q. Describe your hobbies and interests?

Positive things to mention here include:

- Team sports;

- Individual sports;

- Walking and mountaineering;

- Cycling;

- Swimming;

- Yoga or Pilates;

- Camping and orienteering;

- Playing a musical instrument.

Q. Are you currently employed either full-time or part-time?

If you are already employed then this is a positive thing to tell the interview panel. If you are not employed, either full-time or part-time, then you will need to provide reasons why you have not taken on any form of employment. If you are still in education then there is no reason why you cannot find part-time work. If it is simply a case that you have not been able to find any form of employment then you might wish to consider finding a voluntary role to carry out as this will give you invaluable experience of working with others.

Q. What did you used to do during your school holidays?

A great response to this interview question is to say that you were always active during the school holidays and playing team sports. You love the outdoors and would often go camping with your friends or go off on expeditions. If you enjoy travelling then this is a good thing to tell the interview panel as it will demonstrate that you are comfortable with being away from home in different environments.

Q. Have you ever travelled? If so, where and when did you go and what did you gain from the experience(s)?

Q. What are your future ambitions or plans?

Here's how I would personally answer this question:

"My current ambition is to secure a job as an Officer with the Army. I then want to excel during the training course, learn as much as possible about the role and organisation and also be accepted by my peers. With regard to future ambitions, I would very much like to spend many years in the Army and progress through the ranks. However, it would be important for me to become competent and

proficient in each role before I considered applying for promotion and to also have the backing and recommendation of my Senior Officers.

In brief, I see my future and ambitions centred on a career in the Army."

EMPLOYMENT

If you have no experience in a work related role to date, how do you know that you will be a good employee for the Army? Make sure you have some work experience under your belt, even if it's part time work or charity work. Try to also provide examples of responsibilities during each work role and any managerial experience too. These will all work in your favour.

Q. What responsibilities have you had during any jobs you have undertaken to date?

Q. Why did you leave each job?

It is far better to say that you left a job to find a new challenge than you left because the pay was poor or the job was uninspiring! Here's a good response to this question:

"I decided to leave this particular job because I felt I had learnt all that I could within the role. I thoroughly enjoyed my time with the employer but it was time for me to leave and seek a new and more demanding challenge."

Q. Did you complete any courses or gain any qualifications during each job?

Q. Who did you have to communicate with in each job?

Q. Were you part of a team or did you work alone?

Q. What were your appraisals like?

If your appraisals were good then this is a great thing to tell the panel. However, most people usually have an area of improvement identified during an appraisal. If this relates to you, make sure you tell the panel that you always take on-board the feedback provided by your line manager, and also that you implemented an 'action plan' for improvement immediately following your appraisal. Remember that one of the key attributes for joining the Army is the ability to 'learn and develop'.

MOTIVATIONAL QUESTIONS

Q. Why do you want to join the Army? Have you considered the RAF or the Royal Navy?

Q. What specifically attracts you to the Army?

Q. When did you first want to join and has anyone influenced you in your decision to join?

Nobody should have influenced you to join – the decision should be your own following extensive research into the role and the organisation.

Q. Who have you talked to about a career in the Army?

Q. How many visits have you had to the Armed Forces Careers Office?

It is better to say that you had five visits than just the one! This will show how keen and enthusiastic you are about joining and absorbing all there is to know about the Army.

Q. Have you previously attended AOSB? If you have, what have you done to improve on last time?

If you have been to AOSB before and failed, it is imperative that you provide details about how you have worked on your weak areas.

If you attend the AOSB for a second time without having improved, there is very little chance of you passing. For example, if you failed the first time due to your fitness levels (or lack of them), provide comprehensive details of the work you have been doing in order to improve.

Q. What contact have you had with the Army? Have you visited any establishments or spoken to any serving members?

Visiting Army establishments prior to going to AOSB is a positive thing. There are many different establishments you could attend, including museums!

Q. Are there any disadvantages for you joining?

There should be no disadvantages to you joining the Army.

Q. What do your family and friends think of you joining?

Q. What branch of the Army have you applied for and for what reasons?

Q. Would you consider any other branches of the Army other than the one(s) you have chosen?

Here's how I would personally answer this interview question:

"I have been working very hard toward my selected branch and I have my heart set on joining it. Having said that, my priority lies with joining the Army and if the selectors deem I would be more suited to another branch then I would seriously consider it. Having said that, I do very much want to join my chosen branch and I hope that with continued hard-work and dedication this will become a reality."

Q. What research have you carried out during your preparation for joining the Army?

You obviously need to demonstrate that you have carried out lots of research about the Army, the different branches, your training and current operations.

Q. Would you consider a Non-Commissioned role if you were unsuccessful at AOSB?

Here's how I would personally answer this question:

"My aim is to become an Officer with the Army and therefore I would not want to join as a Soldier. If I was unsuccessful at this attempt then I would want to go away and work hard on my identified weak areas. I strongly believe I have the right qualities, attributes and determination levels to become a competent Officer and I won't give up until I prove to the assessors that I have the potential to become part of their team."

Q. What qualities are required in order to become an Army Officer?

Defend your branch choice as much as possible. In order to be capable of achieving this, you will need to know it inside out. Make sure you research key information about your chosen branch/career.

KNOWLEDGE OF THE ARMY

Q. Tell me what you know about the history of the Army?

Q. What training will you undergo as an Officer?

Q. Do you think you will have any problems or face any challenges during Initial Officer Training?

Q. Have you learnt anything about other branches of the Army? For example, if you are applying to join the Army Air Corp, what do you know about the Engineering section?

Q. Tell me what you know about the different aircraft and tanks that we use in the Army?

Q. Tell me what you know about the different weapons that we use in the Army?

Q. Tell me what you know about the different types of weapons that are carried on our aircraft?

Q. How would you feel about going to war?

Q. Where are the UK and overseas bases of the Army?

Q. Whereabouts in the world is the Army operating right now?

CURRENT AFFAIRS QUESTIONS

Current affairs are a very important area of your preparation. You must carry out plenty of research in relation to current affairs. Not only will you need it during the interview(s), but it will also assist you during the essay element of the AOSB.

Here are a few important tips to help you research current affairs effectively:

Tip 1 – Be careful what paper(s) you read. The type of paper you read will reflect you as a person. If you tell the interviewer that you are an avid reader of the Sun or the Daily Star, you may not be officer material. In the build up to AOSB, try reading the Times, or another quality newspaper.

Tip 2 – I would strongly recommend that you subscribe to 'The Week'. This is a fantastic journal that will break down the week's stories for you. It will save having to buy lots of different newspapers.

You can subscribe to the week at the following website:

WWW.THEWEEK.CO.UK

Tip 3 – Consider reading the Economist. Once again, this is a quality journal that will provide you with lots of current affairs information.

You can subscribe to the Economist at the following website:

WWW.ECONOMIST.COM

Tip 4 – Don't just research affairs that are relevant to the Army or the Armed Forces in general. Other topics are just as important!

The purpose of the current affairs section of the AOSB interview is designed to assess how informed you are about current global affairs. You should have a general view on each subject and have an understanding of why the issue is important. Try to have a general view of the whole world with knowledge of a number of issues and events.

Use this format to help you research news and current affairs events:

- What is the subject?

- Why is it significant?

- What is your opinion on it?

SAMPLE CURRENT AFFAIRS QUESTIONS

Q. Take me on a tour of the world and tell me what's caught your eye in the news recently.

Q. Tell me about six current affairs from abroad and six from home.

Q. Tell me about a news story from each continent.

USEFUL WEBSITES

We have provided you with a list of useful websites to help you in your preparation for passing the army officer interview.

BBC News

WWW.BBC.CO.UK/NEWS

The Times Online

WWW.TIMESONLINE.CO.UK

NATO (North Atlantic Treaty Organisation

WWW.NATO.INT

Ministry of Defence

WWW.MOD.UK

Army

WWW.ARMY.MOD.UK

Royal Navy

WWW.ROYALNAVY.MOD.UK

Royal Air Force

WWW.RAF.MOD.UK

FINAL INTERVIEW TIPS

- Research key affairs from across the world.

- Have a broad knowledge of current affairs.

- Research affairs that have happened in the last twelve months.

- Focus in detail on events in the last six months.

- Select six topics for 'home' affairs (e.g. the budget, gang culture).

- Select six topics for 'away' affairs. Make sure that you use examples from right across the world.

- Gauge an opinion of each affair (you will need to be able to argue your point).

- Know key facts: people, numbers, locations etc.

- A firm handshake demonstrates a lot about your character.

- Be to the point and concise (don't waffle).

- Hold even eye contact with each boarding officer.

- Avoid hesitations such as "erm, ah, umm etc".

- Don't use slang.

- Sit up straight and don't slouch.

- Be confident but not overly so!

- Learn the dates and events listed on your application form.

- Make yourself stand out – do something different.

- Be aware of your weaknesses.

- Identify your strengths.

- Think before you speak.

A FEW FINAL WORDS

You have now reached the end of the guide and no doubt you will be ready to start preparing for the Army Officer selection process. Just before you go off and start on your preparation, consider the following.

The majority of candidates who pass the selection process have a number of factors in common. These are as follows:

1. They believe in themselves.

The first factor is self-belief. Regardless of what anyone tells you, you can pass the AOSB and you can achieve high scores. Just like any job of this nature, you have to be prepared to work hard in order to be successful. The biggest piece of advice I can give you is to concentrate on matching the assessable qualities that form part of the scoring criteria. These would be at the forefront of my mind if I were going through selection right now. Make sure you have the self-belief to pass the selection process and fill your mind with positive thoughts.

2. They prepare fully.

The second factor is preparation. Those people who achieve in life prepare fully for every eventuality and that is what you must do when you apply to become an Officer with the Army. Work very hard and especially concentrate on your weak areas. Within this guide I have spoken a lot about preparation. Identify the areas that you are weak on and go all out to improve them.

3. They persevere.

Perseverance is a fantastic word. Everybody comes across obstacles or setbacks in their life, but it is what you do about those setbacks that is important. If you fail at something, ask yourself 'why' have I failed? This will allow you to improve for next time and if you keep improving and trying, success will eventually follow. Apply this same method of thinking when you apply to join the Army as an Officer.

4. They are self-motivated.

How much do you want to join the Army? Do you want it, or do you really want it? When you apply to join you should want it more than anything in the world. Your levels of self-motivation will shine through when you walk into the AFCO and when you attend the Army Officer Selection Board. For the weeks and months leading up to the selection process, be motivated as best you can and always keep your fitness levels up as this will serve to increase your levels of motivation.

Work hard, stay focused, and secure your dream career!

ARMY OFFICER COURSE

- A 1 day army officer training course;

- Learn how to pass each stage of the Army selection process;

- The course will cover the application form, the assessment centre and the interview.

www.ArmyOfficerCourse.co.uk

NEED A LITTLE EXTRA HELP WITH JOINING THE UK ARMED FORCES?

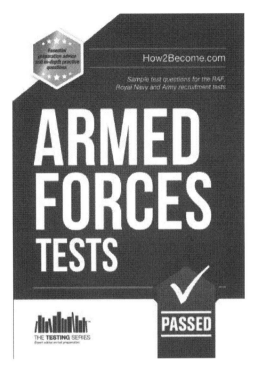

How2Become have created two other FANTASTIC guides to help you prepare for the UK Army selection process.

These exciting guides are filled with essential facts, to ensure that your preparation is thorough, and that you are completely ready for the process ahead. With our help, you can secure your dream career today.

FOR MORE INFORMATION ON OUR ARMY GUIDES, PLEASE CHECK OUT THE FOLLOWING:
WWW.HOW2BECOME.COM

WHY NOT TAKE A LOOK AT OUR OTHER ARMY GUIDES!

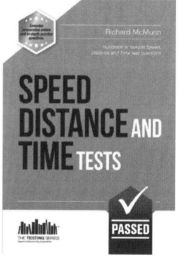

FOR MORE INFORMATION ON OUR ARMY GUIDES, PLEASE CHECK OUT THE FOLLOWING:

WWW.HOW2BECOME.COM

Get Access To

FREE

Psychometric

Tests

www.MyPsychometricTests.co.uk

Printed in Great Britain
by Amazon